THE ABANDONED WESTERN CASCADE MOUNTAIN RAILROAD TUNNELS

MARQUES VICKERS

The Abandoned Western Cascade Mountain
Railroad Tunnels and 1910 Wellington Avalanche

The Photography of Marques Vickers

**MARQUIS PUBLISHING
HERRON ISLAND, WASHINGTON**

Version 1.3

Published by Marquis Publishing
Herron Island, Washington USA

Vickers, Marques, 1957

The Abandoned Western Cascade Mountain Railroad Tunnels and 1910 Wellington Avalanche

Dedicated to my daughters Charline and Caroline

Table of Contents

Abandoned Artifacts and Ghostly Reminders

The creation of the train routes through the Western Washington Cascade Mountains proved a monumental challenge. The conflict arose between the engineering capabilities of man and the treacherous topography and inclement weather of the region.

The nine miles of track connecting the towns of Stevens Pass, Wellington and Scenic, Washington ultimately proved a failure for the Great Northern Railway. The Iron Goat Trail that retraces the former routing is a popular hiking destination. The trailhead is easily accessible by car. The well-maintained path leads you through traces of two ghost towns that were obliterated by avalanche.

In the last decade of the nineteenth century, railroads were the primary mode of transportation for transcontinental passenger travel and freight. Previously isolated and inaccessible portions of the country became connected. Geographical impediments were merely obstacles to overcome. As profits swelled, ambitious and bold routings were designed and realized. During the 1890s, construction innovations enabled greater travel and more direct routes. These projects, employing tunneling and snow sheds, began lining the mountainous stretches immediately past Stevens Pass on the route to the Everett and Seattle stations.

Immigrant laborers cleared the hillsides of mammoth trees. They drilled and blasted rock to create a flat grade. Camps were required for the hundreds of workers to maintain the tracks and keep them operational during the winter snows. Snowdrifts on the mountains often piled as high as 25 feet on either side of the tracks, creating artificial canyons and muffling warning noises. Snow slides often trapped and

5

delayed trains for long periods of time until snowplows and large crews could manually shovel the paths.

Crossing the Western Cascades in winter was a daunting trek. Initially, the lush forests offered protection from avalanche perils. Over time, logging, grade construction and fires cleared the landscape making them vulnerable to heavy snow slides. Sparks emitted by the passing trains often ignited the forest.

Along the Stevens Pass corridor between Wellington and Scenic, eight snowsheds and tunnels protected trains from the perilous conditions. Under these shelters, trains and passengers were considered safe. Exposed areas made trains susceptible to danger.

Construction on the snowsheds began in 1893. Each were framed with untreated Douglas fir, hemlock and Pacific Silver Fir beams and reinforced with concrete. The interior of the structures however, created residual problems, often trapping smoke and hindering visibility. The summer heat caused the timbers to become dry and less resistant to sparks from passing trains.

Maintenance costs skyrocketed during the winter months. The massive snows and periodic avalanches sometimes caused lengthy closures and worse fatalities. Derailments, destroyed bridges and the human risk factor made the decision to abandon the menacing stretch an economic necessity by 1921. Construction began in December 1925 of an alternate lower elevation extended tunnel route that remains today. Upon its completion, the doomed stretch between Stevens Pass, Wellington and Scenic was abandoned to the elements.

The snowsheds and tunnels remain as relics. They have continued a slow but steady deterioration, crumbling and becoming defaced with graffiti. Their existence is a threat to the curious who enter due to unpredictable falling debris and flash flooding.

Danger aside, imagination is stirred when entering these relics. On envisions a bygone era where the speed of transport was relative. A voyage by cross-country train does not match the speed required by contemporary travelers.

In their silence and emptiness, the vacant tunnels and snow sheds resemble tombs depicting casualties of time.

An irony persists that the most accessible remnants of this era were constructed within the decade following the most devastating catastrophe in American railroad history.

Wellington Avalanche

In 1910, Wellington was a miniscule mountain town that existed exclusively due to the Great Northern Railway. Constructed in 1893, the town was the operational headquarters for tunnel construction, tunnel electrification and general maintenance along the line. It was also an important coal, water and rest stop for trains on route to Everett, Seattle and Tacoma.

The infamous avalanche happened on March 1, 1910. Due to the ferocity of the storms, two trains were delayed for a week. The trains, #25 and #27, carried approximately 100 passengers bound for Seattle, had originated from the St. Paul, Minnesota depot. The pace had lurched forward until travel became impossible at the Wellington station on Thursday, February 24th. Their ominous fate seemed predestined when one of the previous dining shacks, at which they'd eaten on February 22nd, collapsed from accumulated snows and killed the cook and his helper.

The journey mirrored a literary voyage of the damned. Hillsides of snow, trees and rocks frequently slid over the tracks around Windy Point, near Scenic a few miles in advance.

The late February 1910 snowstorm was relentless and persisting.

Rotary snowplows attempted to clear tracks, but the task proved impossible for emergency crews due to diminishing coal supplies and the intensity of the storm. Equipment regularly broke and workers were losing a calculated race against time to clear the passage. The rotary plows eventually were depleted of coal and the demoralized shovelers quit working. By Saturday, February 26th, passengers remained stranded in Wellington, rationing food and completely cut off from outside communications.

There were forewarnings of disaster. The echoes of avalanches originating from surrounding mountains were audible. Passengers were restless and concerned that their train was at risk in the exposed Wellington rail yard. They demanded their train be moved back into a protective tunnel.

Disregarding their request, the Train Superintendent James O'Neil assured them of their safety. He refused to authorize the move.

He had confidence that his work crews could break through with a sustained effort and knew of no precedence for landslides in the flatlands of Wellington. He resisted the decision to relocate the trains into the protective confines of the tunnel due to his fear of smoke asphyxiation of the passengers.

Still, O'Neill was not oblivious to the risk. During his two and a half year tenure, he would relocate his private coach during winter into the Stevens Pass region and reside there. He personally supervised operations during storms and snow slides and claimed that before February 23, 1910, he had put more than 4000 trains through the mountain route with none being delayed in excess of 24 hours.

On Monday, February 28th, seven disgruntled male passengers followed a treacherous path down an avalanche chute to Scenic, One returned back to Wellington due to the severity of the conditions. Other passengers had planned to follow their example the next day.

The storm shifted. Rain, lightning and thunder replaced snowdrifts.

A direct lightning hit in the early morning of Tuesday, March 1st, triggered an avalanche. Abruptly colossal layers of snow slid down the mountainside. There was no warning for Trains #25 and #27. The force was devastating and excessive.

The two trains were hurled into a gulch and the frozen waters of the Tye River far below. The train depot, fifteen train cars, coaches, a half dozen locomotives, engines and sheds were buried and tossed indiscriminately.
Wellington residents and surviving train personnel immediately began digging for survivors.

One railroad employee hiked first to Windy Point and then Scenic to report the disaster. A relief train of fifty doctors, nurses, sheriffs and coroners departed from Everett arriving at Scenic. The emergency band struggled uphill through deep snows to arrive at the morgue that was once Wellington.

Amidst the continuance of the storm, victims were lifted from the gulch and wreckage. Seven days of grueling search yielded 95 cadavers. The railroad tracks were finally cleared for passage on March 12th. The dead were transported to Everett. The trains resumed their regular service. The spring snowmelt revealed a final body bringing the confirmed death total to 96.

The notoriety of the disaster prompted the town of Wellington to be renamed Tye. The change mattered little. The annual danger posed by the passage route would ultimately make the continuation of the town unfeasible.

THE ROAD TO WELLINGTON

WELLINGTON VIEWED FROM HIGHWAY 2

TYE RIVER

WELLINGTON SNOW SHED

WELLINGTON TUNNEL

WINDY POINT SNOW SHED

INSIDE WINDY POINT TUNNEL

Author, photographer and visual artist Marques Vickers was born in 1957 in Vallejo, California. He graduated from Azusa Pacific University in Los Angeles and became the Public Relations and Executive Director for the Burbank, California Chamber of Commerce between 1979-84.

Professionally, he has operated travel, apparel, wine, rare book and publishing businesses. His paintings and sculptures have been exhibited in art galleries, private collections and museums in the United States and Europe. He has previously lived in the Burgundy and Languedoc regions of France and currently lives in the South Puget Sound region of Western Washington.

He has written and published over one hundred books spanning a diverse variety of subjects including true crime, international travel, social satire, wine production, architecture, history, fiction, auctions, fine art, poetry and photojournalism.

He has two daughters, Charline and Caroline who reside in Europe.

Made in the USA
Coppell, TX
01 December 2019